GOOD
GRIEF
RITUALS

OTHER HEALING COMPANIONS

How to Forgive When You Don't Know How
How to Break the Vicious Circles in Your Relationships

A HEALING COMPANION

GOOD
GRIEF
RITUALS
Tools for Healing

Elaine Childs-Gowell, A.R.N.P., Ph.D.

PHOTOGRAPHS BY RICHARD GUMMERE

Station Hill Press

Published by Station Hill Press, Barrytown, New York, 12507.
Cover design by Susan Quasha.
Text design by Victoria G. Heemstra.

Distributed by The Talman Company, 131 Spring Street, New York, New York
10012.

Libary of Congress Cataloging-in-Publication Data

Childs-Gowell, Elaine.
    Good grief rituals : tools for healing / Elaine Childs-Gowell.
        p.   cm.
    Includes bibliographical references.
    ISBN 0-88268-118-4 (pbk.)
    1. Grief — Problems, exercises, etc. 2. Loss (Psychology) —
Problems, exercises, etc. 3. Ritual — Psychology. I. Title.
BF575.G7C47 1992
155.9'37 — dc20   92-27479
                                                CIP

Manufactured in the United States of America.

CONTENTS

ACKNOWLEDGMENTS

I am deeply grateful to the following persons who made my own grief process imperative and meaningful. First, to my spiritual friend and husband Dick Gowell whose own pain and grief from his World War II experiences I shared intimately. Next, to those who were my psychotherapists and mentors, and to my clients who have been my teachers throughout the years during which I was growing to the state of wisdom and light that I have now achieved. To my friends, family, and all those who shared in developing this tool for dealing with the grief process with me over the years. THANK YOU ALL.

INTRODUCTION

Open the door: There is magic under the teapot, in your shoestring . . . and in the wind outside, chanting to you.

Marina Medici

This is a book of tools for life. The tools in this book are called healing rituals. If these rituals are used as directed, they will allow you to become complete with most, if not all, of the grief issues that you still have facing you. The book provides a set of skills for anyone who has experienced a **loss** of any kind in his/her life. Whether the loss is recent or seemingly archaic, the process will be of value to you. In short, these rituals are given as a set of tools for those who are currently grieving, as well as for those who have "old" grief issues. The book provides rituals for dealing with **forgiveness** and, ultimately, with **gratitude**.

WHO NEEDS TO CREATE GRIEF RITUALS

Grief has a quality of healing in it that is very deep because we are forced to a depth of emotion that is usually below the threshold of our awareness.
Stephen Levine

There are very few people who would not benefit from this process. Most of us in one way or another fit into the categories mentioned next. Adult children of dysfunctional families, adult children of alcoholics, victims of incest and assault, disaster victims, such as War Veterans and their families, persons whose families moved a lot when they were kids such as service families ("Army Brats" and ministers' kids), anyone who has lost a pet or had a car wrecked, or even people whose parents got rid of favorite toys, stuffed animals, etc., without their explicit consent and involvement in the decision, will have a grief issue to deal with and have to come to a clear place with respect to the loss.

If you are a widow, a widower, have lost a lover, a pet, or a dear friend; if you have made a major change in your life — lost or gained a job, moved to a new home, or whatever the loss — the Rituals this book provides will serve you throughout your life in helping you to deal with the **feelings** aroused by these events. The Rituals and tools provided in this book are for anyone at all who has experienced a loss of any kind. We have little choice about grief; we are going to be facing it no matter how our life unfolds. If we have the life skills to do this with grace, we will be happier.

All real living is meeting. Meeting is not in time and space, but space and time in meeting.

Martin Buber

WAR IS EVERYONE'S GRIEF

No one on the planet can escape the grief of war. It touches us all, whether or not we're willing to acknowledge it. Words do not begin to describe the depth of my own despair and deep grieving for the suffering of military combatants — and for their victims. My husband was a World War II Veteran and had the PTSD (Post-Traumatic Stress Disorder) symptoms all of his adult life. Nineteen years old when he entered the Navy in World War II, he was never able to stop the flashbacks or deal with the pain of the experience until shortly before he died. The legacy of the unspeakable traumas he experienced, which he passed on to his family in a myriad of ways, remain ingrained in all of us.

I have only deep compassion for those who, like him, did things and witnessed events that scarred them and their close associates in life. If you think you have no grief issues, think again. We cannot escape My Lai or Belsen or the devastation to man and nature created across most of the planet by the group Eisenhower called the Military Industrial Complex. We have so much to grieve for and so much more to do about our grief than we realize.

STAGES OF GRIEF

Imagination is more important than knowledge.

Albert Einstein

Everyone grieves. When we have a grief issue to deal with, we tend to go through four stages (according to Elizabeth Kübler-Ross). In the first stage, we deny the event; second, we bargain to have the situation changed; next, we become very mad, sad, and scared; and, finally, we reconcile to the event and experience forgiveness and gratitude. Grieving is a *necessary* and *important* event that will reoccur for each and every one of us throughout our lives. If we take responsibility and deal with the feelings, then we will not be dragging it along and plugging up our capacity for joy. As I move through life, I experience many losses. That is the nature of life on this planet. Sometimes the loss is a small one, and sometimes it is a very big one. Sometimes the loss is an illusion that I've held for many years. Whatever it is that I have lost (or must give up), I **must grieve**. I must forgive myself and the person and events about whom I have experienced a loss. It is imperative that

I take responsibility for the impact the loss has made on my life and that I take the time to deal DAILY with the feelings that arise as a result of the loss. I must do this until I am completely clear of the archaic feelings and unfinished business I have with the person or the event that troubles me.

I say "must." The reason is that I have discovered that this is one of life's imperatives. *If I do not do my grieving about the old hurts and insults, then, when I am faced with a here and now grief experience, I will end up having to dredge up all that old energy along with the current experience.* When my mother died, I was surprised and pleased to find that my grieving for her was quite easy because, some years before she died, I had done my grief work vis à vis the hard times we had had together when I was growing up. Her death produced a clear, clean, and present grief for me.

Because the sage always chooses to confront difficulties, he is never stuck with the experience of them.
Lao Tzu

It was also important for me that I had done my grief work because, when a major loss such as this occurred in my life, I had fewer stressors lurking in my psyche to cause me psychological pain. Moreover, there was less chance of a psychosomatic disorder to accompany the time of actual grief and loss.

Now stop reading, and write down as many of your grief and loss issues as come to mind in the present moment.

LOSS

Within each of us lies the power of our consent to health and to sickness, to riches and to poverty, to freedom and to slavery. It is we who control these, and not another.

Richard Bach

We are all products of our growing up, and we carry within us a Child-part who continues to feel as strongly as we did when we were that age. Those of us who deny the Child within may expect to have psychosomatic disorders and/or symptoms of the Post-Traumatic Stress Disorder (PTSD) as our bodies and psyches try to deal subconsciously instead of openly with the stress of the unexpressed grief. PTSD is what people experience after coming out of a major disaster experience such as war, fire, a hurricane, a shipwreck. Anytime that I deny my feelings my body will react with old feeling states, and when there is a sufficient backlog of those old feeling states, some part of my body will overreact. This will be manifested in what is my "target organ," and I will have a stomachache, colitis, skin conditions, and a myriad of disorders now known to have a psychological basis. Some people will overreact and make a big deal out of some minor event in their life.

At this point you could list the bodily problems you have now in your life.

DENIAL – WHO ME?

Our American culture made a virtue of our living only as extroverts. We discouraged the inner journey, the quest for a center, so we lost our center and had to find it again.

Anais Nin

Well, now YOU might say that you don't have anyone to forgive, or you are quite sure you have no grief issues. You may indeed be such a fortunate person! I have never met anyone who did not have a grief issue of one kind or another, and, if such exists, how unhuman and, indeed, unfortunate for them! It is crucial that we consciously acknowledge the universality of the need to grieve. Grieving is not in response only to those in my life who have died. Grief involves every person, object, or incident from which I have walked away with a sense of being *incomplete*. The loss may have been of a pet, or a favorite object, a major life or love change, a new job, etc. Even if I disliked that job, there is still grief to be expressed about it! It is really important to me to complete all interactions in my life. It is important to be **complete** with every negative or uncomfortable event, situation, or person I have ever encountered, no matter how long ago it was.

CAN'T GO BACK THAT FAR?

Oh my! you say, I can't go back that far! Yes I can! And if I don't, I will find that the old grief will tear at me in some way and create problems for me when my body gets old and less resilient. I have no question but that heart disease, coronary artery disease, and many other disorders are directly related to the unfinished business of life. Norman Cousins has stated that there is now enough evidence to show that tissue-damaging chemicals known as catecholamines are released into the heart muscle when we are unduly stressed. Obviously, as the body ages, unpleasant and unwelcome flashbacks become riskier.

FLASHBACKS

Another important motivation to do grief work is dealing with flashbacks. Flashbacks are unexpected and often triggered by a current event, a smell, a sound, or a scene in the present that reminds me of the old event. If I do not do my grief work, I am more subject to these unpleasant, ill-timed, and often unwelcome experiences. So I have to take time out to recall and release the past experience. The careful and meticulous experiencing of the grief process becomes a form of preventive medicine. It doesn't do me any good to go on denying the impact of these past events if I wish to live a long and healthy life.

Sit down before fact like a little child, and be prepared to give up every preconceived notion, follow humbly wherever and to whatever abyss Nature leads, or you shall learn nothing.

T.H. Huxley

TAKE TIME TO GRIEVE

Those who wish to sing always find a song.

Swedish proverb

The careful experiencing of the grief process is a form of preventive medicine. It does me good to deal with the impact of those past events. I do wish to live a long and healthy life. How much better that I take time now, when I have the energy and the life in me to face some of the old music. Each time I have spent working on myself, freeing myself of the old grief, has given me more time in the years since to enjoy myself fully and completely. Each time I have released an old grief, I have felt more joy in my life. I have learned that if I do not deal with the grief issue, it clouds and overshadows my whole day and even creeps into my dreams. When I do deal with the issues, I find myself free until the next slot of time I have set aside for this process.

Time is the gift we have been given to come to terms with our mortality.

SPIRITUAL GROWTH

God is at home. It is we who have gone out for a walk.

Meister Eckhart

There is another even more profound reason for me to stop my denial and get on with my grief process. That is the issue of spiritual growth. Each piece of unfinished grief represents a tie to this earth plane and to this body. Any effort to move to the higher planes of the spirit may be hampered so long as I am encumbered by old grief. I must forgive myself and all of those with whom I have been involved over the years, so I can become clear. When I am clear of my old grief, I will feel the forgiveness deep in my body and I will feel a deep gratitude for the person I have forgiven. When this happens, I will feel the **light** within me, and with the light I can move onwards on my Path.

RITUALS

Rituals are not the path. They are the reminder that there is a path.

Emmanuel

Rituals are specifically designed actions, whether physical or mental, that are used to *change our perception of reality*. Often, I begin and perform a Ritual before I am aware of the meaning within it. Every Ritual that has full and deep meaning for the participant **will result in a transformation of personality** and **will feel like magic.** Rituals help me to realize and utilize energy flows — remember feelings are energy. A Ritual can be as simple as lighting a candle or filling a vase with flowers or thinking a special thought. In the Ritual you create a small event in order to reflect bigger events in your life. A grief Ritual will allow you to move energy and experience a transformation of your relationship to the lost one. All Rituals contain a preparatory phase, an experiencing phase, and an ending, or closing, phase. Each phase has symbols and meanings that are relevant to that phase, to the subsequent phases, and to the outcome you desire.

At this point you might thumb through the rest of this book until something catches your eye: spend five minutes doing that Ritual.

RITUALS AND RITUALS

I like to think of Ritual (big R) as different from
ritual (little r) in this way. The "littler" rituals are the
ones we do everyday without thinking, like saying
hello to the bus driver or waving to the engineer on
the train passing by. "Big R" Rituals are the ones
into which we have put some thought and in which
the repetitive nature of the processes through which
we go are symbolic on a deep psychological level for
us. The way in which Rituals work for us is that we
are making use of energy in a variety of ways. They
help us to clarify aspects of our lives that may not be
clear to us. When we create a Ritual, we are acting
out either in imagination or in actuality the **micro-
cosm** of what we wish for in the **macrocosm**. It is
helpful to suspend judgement when we do our Rituals because we need to give our whole attention to
the process of the Ritual, and to its precise aspects.
A simple thing like lighting a candle, planting a
bush, brushing our teeth can become a Ritual that can
help us release the bound energy in our psyche and
give us a feeling of peace from what was causing us

pain before the Ritual. Rituals help us walk in balance and in reverence.

When you are clear about the purpose of the Ritual go through the steps of preparation:

ONE: **Gathering the materials** for the Ritual.

TWO: **Preparing yourself inwardly** (meditation, fasting, or some form of purification).

THREE: **Do the Ritual itself.** You can be as elaborate or as simple as you wish; if the elements are **meaningful** to you in a deep energetic way, the Ritual will succeed in its purpose.

Now Bless Yourself in the following way: Get a candle, a bowl of water, and some sage or incense. Sit quietly, light the candle, and let all tension slip away from your body. Put your fingers in the water and touch them to your forehead, saying to yourself out loud, "Bless my understanding so that I may be here fully." Next touch the water to your eyes and say,

"Bless my vision so that I may see with clarity."
Touch your mouth with the water and say, "Bless my
mouth so that I may speak with truth." Continue to
do this with ears, heart, head, other parts of your
body or of your consciousness. Reflect for a moment
on what you have just done. Blow out the candle and
empty the bowl, washing it, and **feel the completion
of your Self-Blessing Ritual.**

> *This is what I want to happen: that our earth mother*
> *may be clothed in ground corn four times over;*
> *that frost flowers cover her entirely;*
> *that the mountain pines far away over there*
> *may stand close to each other in the cold;*
> *that the weight of snow crack some branches!*
> *In order that the country be this way*
> *I have made my prayer sticks into something alive.*
>
> **Zuni**

REVENGE WORK

Your life is not your
master. It is your child.
Emmanuel

I have tired of **telling** people what to do and how to do it each time they are faced with a grief issue. I have therefore developed an instruction sheet that a person can take home and do as homework. If you are willing to agree to follow the instructions, then you will make a healing contract as part of your grieving process.

A contract is an agreement with yourself that defines a behavior on your part, such as: "I will brush my teeth everyday." Euphemistically, it is sometimes called "taking out a contract on —." This gives the Child within a sense of power since one of the major blocks to grieving is the mourner's need for "revenge" against the lost person whom they are grieving. Until you have dealt with the sense of outrage and the wish to "get even," it is impossible to forgive the other person, or the circumstances, or finally even yourself.

The taboo against "vengeance work" thus often blocks us from being able to deal with the whole range of emotions involved in full and proper grieving. Because "getting revenge" is one of the taboos in this culture, it is subject to superstitious thinking.

The taboo has to do with the *intent*: if your intent is to heal the rift, then the vengeance work is appropriate; if the intent is ultimately to destroy, then it is not appropriate. (See "Resolving the Loss…" below.)

Another reason you may be unable to do your grief work is the mistaken belief that you must protect the person against whom you have a grievance. You may believe, as many people do, that the object of your vengeance could not stand your feelings, even if they are not in any way present or may even be dead. This belief is another superstition. You can think about the beliefs you have that do not work for you and jot them down.

ATTACHMENT AND BROKEN BONDS

The *grief process* is based on the theory of attachment and bonding.* Whether there was full attachment to the object or person or there was failure to attach, there will still be a sense of loss and a reaction to that loss. I have discovered that I have three options for dealing with my reaction to the loss:

1. I may ignore (deny) the loss, and go on as if nothing happened. Many individuals who do this will pay the psychosomatic price for the choice, later suffering more and more bodily problems. Often these bodily problems are a mystery even to professional persons, and more so to the western medical professionals that are consulted. Eating a healthy diet and living in a healthy environment are part of the preventive picture, and having a healthy internal, psychological environment is the other part that must not be neglected.

* See John Bowlby's *Attachment and Loss* for a discussion of this theory.

2. I may get stuck in the loss cycle and replay the past over and over in what are called flashbacks, "Script scenes," or even karmic debts. The repeated scenes become familiar patterns in our lives, recurring regularly and causing familiar and unwanted pain and perplexity. I call these "gifts from the universe" — as if the universe were telling me that here is an opportunity for me to look at my script and to learn from the recurring pattern, instead of continuing to deny the pain it presents to me.

3. Or, I choose to resolve the loss and find new meaning in my relationship to the person or object or situation to which I was attached. The Grief Process may look somewhat like this chart:

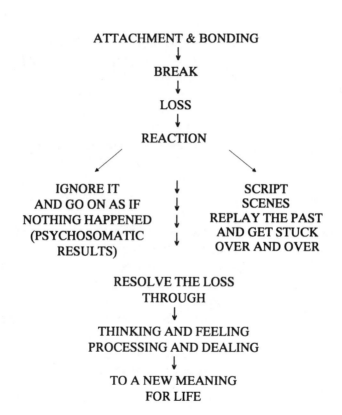

ATTACHMENT & BONDING
↓
BREAK
↓
LOSS
↓
REACTION

IGNORE IT
AND GO ON AS IF
NOTHING HAPPENED
(PSYCHOSOMATIC
RESULTS)

↓
↓
↓
↓

SCRIPT
SCENES
REPLAY THE PAST
AND GET STUCK
OVER AND OVER

RESOLVE THE LOSS
THROUGH
↓
THINKING AND FEELING
PROCESSING AND DEALING
↓
TO A NEW MEANING
FOR LIFE

RESOLVING THE LOSS — THE PROCESS

The best and most beautiful things in the world cannot be seen or even touched. They must be felt with the heart.

Helen Keller

If you are willing to follow this process with a dedication to the final purpose of coming to a new understanding of your relationship to the person or object or situation you are grieving, you will be guaranteed success. Over the years I have used the process myself and have taught it to countless people who have achieved the resolution they sought in their relationships. So, if you are **really committed** (100%) to dealing with your grief and to becoming clear of the pain and discomfort that the unresolved grief causes you—then proceed! First, your contract: **I agree to spend at least 15 minutes and no more than one hour per day doing my grief process Rituals.** When you make this agreement you can then "bracket" your feelings with the knowledge that they will be dealt with at the appropriate time. For those who are in fresh grief times this may not be possible. If you do it more than once or twice a day, you will advance your process, and it's also okay to wait until you are not so overwhelmed.

AN ALTERNATIVE TO DENIAL

*A gem is not polished
without friction
nor is a being realized
without trials.*

Chinese Proverb

For those of you who deny that you have grief work, I suggest the following short exercise (anyone else will find it a useful process, so do it!):

Sit comfortably where you will not be distracted. Take a couple of deep breaths, and let them out slowly, relaxing your body as you do so. Now, imagine that there is a stage in front of you; it can be a small one, or a very large one like the one at the opera house. Imagine that ALL of the people (pets and stuffed animals, too) who have been of some importance to you over your lifetime are on the stage on the left side. Now, on the right side of the stage, put all of the people you have forgiven in your life so far. As you move each person, say **"I forgive you"** and **"I forgive myself"** to that person. If the forgiveness comes from deep within and **is congruent with your whole being**, keep them on the right side of the stage.

Continue to do this for each person who remains on the left until you have examined your relationship

with each one and have forgiven each and every one.
When you are complete — meaning when the process has been completed inside of you — there
should not be a single soul remaining on the left side
of the stage. It is possible to achieve this goal in your
lifetime. If there still is anyone at all on the left side
of the stage, then you have yet to do more "grief
work" with that person. Don't give up if you find a
large number of people still on the left. If you are systematic and organized about this process and continue to do the grief work as outlined below, you will
some day find your stage clear on the left. Make a
list of the people still on the left side of your stage.
Pick one person or event to focus on for the next few
days or weeks.

Now stop the words.
In the center of your chest open the window:
Let the spirits fly in and out.

Rumi

GRIEF PROCESS RITUALS

Be sure that you read this section and the next two sections, "Feelings Are Energy" and "Safe Ways to Act Out Feelings," before starting the work in this section.

The first thing to do is to choose a sacred place to live in.
Tahirasawichi

FIRST: **Make a contract** with yourself or with a friend to do "grief work" daily — **fifteen minutes to one hour per day** for two to three weeks or more. I suggest that you make it a time-limited agreement so that the grief does not spill out into all of your other responsibilities. You should not be thinking about and obsessing over the process. It is important to "bracket" your feelings so that you are not obsessed with them. Keep it clean and do it only during the allotted time.

SECOND: **Sit in a quiet place** and do **one** of the following each time you work:

I: Write **lists** of **Mads / Sads / Scares / Glads** about the loss.

EXAMPLE: I am mad that you went away
I am mad that I am alone
I am mad that I have no control over it

The transformative process, however alien it may seem at first, soon feels irrevocably right. Whatever the initial misgivings, there is no question of com-mittment once we have touched something we thought forever lost — our way home.
Marilyn Ferguson, *The Aquarian Conspiracy*

II: **Write letters in your journal** (do *not* send
them) in which you "let it all hang out" — each
letter to be written to the primary person in the
grief experience. Write "poison pen letters" —
"voodoo notes" — "tales of woe" — "poor me" etc.
Also write love letters, pouring our your love to
the lost one. Do both. This process is to acknowledge the part of you that may be having vengeful
or loving thoughts — it's okay to let that part
have a forum and let yourself acknowledge how
you believe you have been "wronged." **Get it off
your chest! Vengeance work is very important
and must be done in a systematic fashion.** For
those who worry about "thoughts creating
reality" as in Voodoo and in Black Magic — it
has been my experience that the object of the
angry thoughts has to know that it is being done
and has to cooperate in the knowledge in order to
be influenced by it.

The *intent* of the vengeful part of you is to gain relief from the pain of loss. Intent has a lot to do with what we succeed in doing. I have never known harm to come to anyone from doing this — only great good, great relief, great joy, and wonderful healing. Remember that the *deeper intent* of the Ritual grief process (no matter how poisonous it feels) is resolution of — and liberation from — stored negativity.

On the next page you will find a traditional healing Ritual that could be useful.

There is a tradition in North American Indian culture that suggests that if you have a grievous matter to deal with, go out into the woods or to a place where you will be private and dig a hole in the ground near a tree or bush. Pour all of your feelings into that hole. When you are quite satisfied that you have your spirit emptied of the foul stuff, cover the hole and thank the tree for listening and thank Mother Earth for receiving your grief. Then go about your business feeling better about yourself and more connected to the universe. Thank the tree or bush for witnessing your grief process.

III: **Create Affirmations:** Affirmations have been shown to be a very effective way to create a shift on the inner psychic level. Sondra Ray has written several books that outline the affirmation process. The indications are that, if the affirmation is congruent with a deep inner goal, it will be successful. I suggest that you follow this procedure to get the best results:

1: Write the affirmation fifty times or more.

2: On the right side of the page, write all of the negative — the internal — discounts that pop into your mind. Write *all* of them down there.

3: Keep going until the "negative self-talk" ends.

4: Create a new affirmation from the discounts you have written, taking all of your reservations into account.

5: Keep doing this for 21 days or more.

AFFIRMATION	DISCOUNT
I am wanted and loveable.	No I am not!
I am wanted and loveable.	Nobody wants me!
I am wanted and loveable.	This is ridiculous.
I am wanted and loveable.	Who says?
I am now an outstanding artist.	Only Daddy is.
I am now an outstanding artist.	Mom wouldn't like it.
I am now an outstanding artist.	How could I be?

New Affirmation: **"My Mom and Dad now support me in being an outstanding artist."**

IV: **Forgiveness:** Write the two following statements over and over until you are clear and congruent:

    a. I forgive_____for_____.
    b. I forgive myself for_____.

FEELINGS ARE ENERGY

Feelings are so very important, yet there are many of us who won't feel our feelings. If when you are in the process of doing the lists of feelings (i.e., **Mads / Sads / Scares / Glads**), the letters, and the affirmations, and you FEEL a lot of energy in your body, i.e., you **feel** like crying, screaming, shouting, or other action—**Do It!**

Protection: Be sure that you are in a **safe place** so you can act out the energy in your body. **Do not** do any of this in a public place. Many people would be frightened by the force of your feeling work and would not handle it well. You have at least three options: you can do the work in your own home where you are not heard; you can work with a friend; or you can work with your therapist. It is important that your catharsis be connected to someone empathetic — a person, a pet, or a tree.

It is very important to acknowledge the energy in your body and not to gloss over it. This is one of the crucial points where people go into *denial.* Feelings are very taboo in so many families. Some families allow only one feeling; in others, only certain people are allowed the feeling; and in some families *no feelings* are okay.

ENERGY TRANSFORMATION BOX:

Create a box of any size, material, shape. Use this magic box to put the person, event, feeling in while you are not doing your grief work. The box will transform for you some of the problem you are having with your loss.

SAFE WAYS TO ACT OUT FEELINGS

Try one or more of the following exercises in a safe place:

I: **Twist a towel**, or pull one with a friend.

II: **Pound a pillow** or your mattress with your fists, your pelvis, or a tennis racket.

Trust life, my friends. However far afield life seems to take you, this trip is necessary.

Emmanuel

III: **Scream** into a pillow, or in the woods.

IV: **Have a temper tantrum** on your bed or on a mattress.

V: **Go for a long walk or a run,** focusing the feelings in your body movement.

VI: **Dig a hole in the ground** in your backyard or in the woods and pour your feelings out into the ground as described earlier in this book.

VII: **Howl, growl, wail, sing sad songs, laugh, cry, yell, scream or any other kind of noise and movement** that will push you to express how you feel about the loss you have suffered. The interesting

thing about these procedures is that when the feelings are expressed from the core, your mind will be cleared for THINKING about the basic issues involved in your grief.

VIII: **Laugh uproariously, raucously, and with abandon at least once a day**. Laughter does not need a reason. Just do it.

IX: **Dance or paint or draw your feelings** so that they move you and you move them.

X: **Stop suffering about how you have been wronged.** The suffering behavior is one of the ways people avoid working through their feelings and **doing** the necessary feeling work to relieve their tissues of the discomfort. Sometimes it is hard to differentiate **Real Feelings** from **Racket Feelings**.

XI: **Meditate**: take time out to go inside.

XII: **Be any animal that appeals to you**: Act out that animal's way of expressing mad/sad/scared/glad; i.e., Hiss like a raccoon or cat. Growl like a dog.

NOTE: When you express a "Real Feeling" there is a genuine experience of relief. By contrast, a "Racket" leaves you feeling unsatisfied and unclear, and, as is often the case, feeling worse than when you started. Racket feelings are old "familiar feelings" that are substitutes for the actual feeling that has a neuro-physiological basis.*

Becoming conscious is, of course, a sacrilege against nature; it is as though you had robbed the unconscious of something.
C.G. Jung

* Richard Erskine and Marilyn Zalcman give a good description of this difference in the article noted in the reference list at the end of this book.

A RITUAL
BALLOON FANTASY

Close your eyes and imagine you are at a park on a beautiful, sunny, soft spring day. You are walking along and enjoying the soft breezes and the sunshine and feeling so very relaxed. You buy a helium balloon from a vendor and you can feel it gently tugging at your wrist as you tie it on there. Soon you will put in that balloon all of the uncomfortable thoughts, feelings, and experiences in your life that you are ready to give up. Make a list of these and put them in the balloon. When you are ready, slowly untie the balloon from your wrist and let it go with the next breeze. Watch it as it rises gently up, up, and up into the sky until it is completely out of sight. Ask yourself how you feel now, and are you willing to let the balloon take all of that stuff forever? Sometimes we hold onto archaic feelings that do not have their roots in our present life, and we have to go back as far as we need to solve the problem.

MEDITATION IS GOOD MEDICATION

I swim in inner seawater though I do not know how to swim.

Ann Bozarth-Campbell

There are many ways to meditate. Any kind of repeated activity that distracts the busy brain is a form of meditation. For instance a good fast walk, a jog in the park, circle dancing, and many other kinds of activities are meditative. I am going to describe here a standard quiet meditation.

ONE: Sit in a comfortable position with feet flat on floor and hands in lap.

TWO: Focus on your breath and notice each breath as it goes in and out.

THREE: Pick a word, a sound, or an object to look at, and focus your whole attention on one of these. The word can be your name, or "peace," "OM —" or the person for whom you are grieving.

FOUR: As thoughts come into your mind, recognize them as you would a bubble rising in a fish tank; watch the thought and let it go.

FIVE: Maintain this process from 10 to 20 minutes.

SIX: Practice, practice, practice.

ANNIVERSARY DATES

It is very important to remember that there are certain dates that are associated with our experience of loss. The anniversary, the "monthiversary," the particular day of the week sometimes are unexpected times when we remember the person we have lost; and these can be very painful days, especially if we have not prepared ourselves for them. It is important to make note of such dates and plan ahead to do a Grief Ritual so that you will be in charge of the grief experience. It is not unusual for people to have unexpected and unwelcome flashbacks on such dates, and it is better to be ready for them when those special days come around. So plan to do one or more of the Rituals described in this book on the day or the day before the anniversary or "monthiversary." My sister died on the 14th of December a good many years ago. My mother, towards the end of her life, experienced a serious heart attack on the 14th of November and again on the 14th of December and died on the 14th of January. She was of the old school, from the old country, and did not let herself openly acknowledge her grief about my sister's death.

DISCOVERING THE LITTLE CHILD WITHIN

Do not think that there is more in destiny than can be packed into childhood.

Rainer Maria Rilke

This Ritual is a simple one. It requires you to be in a quiet place where you will not be disturbed for five to ten minutes. You allow yourself to get comfortable and to breathe deeply for several breaths. Quiet your breath, and in your mind's eye remember your birthday at five or younger. In your imagination allow yourself to find a photograph of you at one of those ages. Look carefully at the photograph, notice the little child that was you in the picture. See what he/she is wearing. Notice how the hair is fixed and see the expression on the child's face. Now in your imagination bring that child out of the picture to stand in front of you. Reach out your hand and feel the child's hand in yours. Be aware of the child and feel the needs and the personality of the child. Talk with him/her. Take your child to some place of delight like the beach or the zoo, and play together.

Hold your child close to you and ask the child to be with you as you experience your grief about the current loss with which you are now dealing. Feel your feelings fully. It is the child in you who is weeping or raging — give her/him full range. When you are done with this Ritual, thank your Child for being with you and bring him/her inside you so that you will always be able to access his/her energy in your life.

Time present and time past
Are both perhaps present in time future
and time future contained in time past.
                                    T.S. Eliot

INCENSE & HERBS

Many peoples across the world use incense and herbs in their Grief Rituals. The belief is that the smoke rises to the realm of spirit and, conversely, provides a pathway for spirit to come to the person who is using the burning of the herbs for his/her Ritual. It is also believed that the incense smoke provides a pathway for the spirit of the one who has died to go on its way. There is also among many peoples the belief that certain herbs cleanse the space in which they are burned. Here are a couple of Rituals you can use in your grieving process using herbs or incense. The Ritual starts when you go on your quest for the herb or incense. Begin by asking in your mind for the particular herb or incense that will be **right** for you in this particular process. Some of the herbs I have used are sage and rosemary. I have found sandalwood and blue pearl to be the incense I like, and your choice can be just as personal. You may also use a loved one's perfume or cologne.

Go to your quiet place, in your home or in nature, and do or imagine the following:

ONE: Make sure you will not be interrupted and that this time is for you and your grieving process.

TWO: Bring with you a handkerchief or a small piece of cloth, an item which belonged to your loved one, a picture, a container for the incense or herbs, matches to light these, a feather or a fan to spread the smoke, and anything else that seems to you to be an important part of the Ritual.

THREE: To start the Ritual, seat yourself comfortably in front of the cloth or handkerchief that you have spread out, place the items named above on your cloth, light the sage or incense.

FOUR: Access your feelings about the person or the event you are grieving about as you blow three times on the burning incense/sage. As you do this, say, "I miss you," or "I release you," or some other phrase that feels appropriate to you. **Feel Your Feelings. Pour Them Forth.**

FIVE: Using the feather or fan, spread the smoke in the five directions: north, east, south, west, and skyward. As you do this, say three times, "I love you," or "I let you go," or whatever phrase seems right for you.

The finest thing in the world is knowing how to belong to oneself.
Michel de Montaigne

SIX: Stay with your feelings until you are quite sure that you are done this time. Thanking yourself and spirit for the opportunity to let go of your feelings one more time, extinguish the burning incense or herbs. Saying "Thank you" to the herb for helping you, pack your materials and come back to normal waking reality.

NATIVE AMERICAN BELIEFS

With all beings and all things we shall be as relatives.

Sioux proverb

The Native Americans in the Southwest and all of the other Native American groups have many myths and traditional Rituals. They believe in the power of the mind over the body. Their healing Rituals provide great comfort for their peoples, particularly for people who are depressed by mourning. Central to the life view of the Navajo is the view of the universe as an orderly whole. It is made up of people, other living beings, supernaturals, and the nonliving or inert beings like stones. They believe that everything that happens is interrelated. In order to help someone who is ill or depressed, they will call for a "sing." It is called this because singing is one of the main activities. A Ritual will include praying, singing, burning herbs, bodily cleansing, and sand paintings. Rituals have their own story, and they form an integrated part of the total life view of these people. Often the myth has a symbolic solution to the problem that is occurring. These Rituals always involve as many of the family members and others of significance as can be brought together. Symbolic actions involve the participants in giving gifts in the form of prayersticks to the spirits who then are obliged to help the supplicant. Other sorts of symbolic action involve identifying with a key supernatural spirit, such as Changing Woman. Always the symbolic action is getting rid of bad feelings, depression, or sickness. The process is enhanced by taking medicines or doing a "sweat." With these actions, the harmony of mind and body is restored.

One of the Rituals I engage in regularly is going to a "sweat" or taking in a sauna or steam bath. I follow the principles of "Ritual," and unfailingly I come out feeling much more in balance than when I went in. Sometimes, paralleling Native American "medicine" practitioners, contemporary psychotherapists have incorporated myths and Rituals in Western urban life styles. You might adapt the symbolic action mentioned above to your own life and to the materials and facilities available to you. It is possible for you to take charge of your own grief process, calling upon your therapist and/or friends to support you in your Rituals.

Everything is alive; what we call dead is an abstraction.
David Bohm

THE MEDICINE WHEEL
A METAPHOR FOR
THE GRIEF PROCESS

So many things fail to interest us simply because they don't find in us enough surfaces on which to live, and what we have to do is to increase the number of planes in our mind, so that a much larger number of themes can find a plane in it at the same time.

Ortega Y Gasset

The shamanic tradition across many cultures teaches the Medicine Wheel as a way to connect with spirit and to affirm our place in the universe. The Medicine Wheel teaches that each of the four directions has specific tasks for us to attend to in the process of living on the planet and in carrying out growth process. There are power spirits for each direction, and there are special sounds and specific types of meditation prescribed for the passage around the Medicine Wheel. I have found that it is a wonderful and challenging structure through which to do my grief work.

We start in the South, which is the place of the Healer and of the Inner Child of the past where we are called upon to shed our skins as the serpent does, and to be close to the Mother Earth in our process. We can call upon the spirits of the winds of the South to help us deal with our grief issues from the Child part of our personality and from our Inner Healer. In dealing with past griefs, we face the challenge of our family-of-origin. In dealing with the present grief we face the challenge of abandonment and how our inner Child feels about the current loss we are suffering. This is the challenge of the open heart, the full heart, the strong heart, and the clear heart. The mode of healing is storytelling; the type of meditation is lying down; and the music is drumming.

We move to the West, which is the place of the Warrior. It is in this direction that we are called upon to face our deepest fears and to face our mortality. This is where the spirits of the Jaguar and the Grizzly Bear come to teach us about our fears and about our lack of integrity in our lives. In the West is where we deal with the grief around giving up our illusions. We have to deal in this quadrant with our loneliness and our deep terror about never again seeing this one who has died. The sound is from the sticks and bones; the type of meditation is sitting; and the healing salve is silence.

In the North we are offered the task of Mastery. This is the direction of the leader or teacher in us, and here we are given the opportunity to share our knowledge with others. Our guides are the bison and the horse. In this direction we face the deepest rage in our beings about being here. This is where we are "mad at God/Goddess" and where we deal with our fundamental rebellion against being alive, against being here, against having to take responsibility for being alive. In addressing our archaic griefs we are called upon to forgive all of our family members and, ultimately, forgive ourselves. In dealing with current grief issues, we deal with the forgiveness of the person who has died or forgive the aspects of the events that are grieving us, etc. The music for this direction is the rattle; the meditation is the standing meditation; and the healing salve is dancing.

In the East we have the task of creating a Vision for ourselves. This is where we go on a vision quest and ask spirit for help in seeing far and wisely. We are assisted in this direction by the spirit of the Eagle who flies high and can see very far. The healing salve for this direction is singing. We are called upon to use our inner vision, our intuition, and our wisdom, and the meditation for this direction is the walking meditation. When I have done my grieving in this direction I have looked at what I need to do in the other directions so that I can free my energy to be fully committed and fully present in my Vision. My present grief work addresses the current loss in terms of how it affects my accomplishing my Vision.

So, since the Medicine Wheel is a circle, we can start anywhere in it and do it over and over again as we move through the spiral of life. We are challenged to face our feelings in each direction and to do something about releasing the energy we carry with those feelings so we can move on in our personal growth and find our energy freed to create our Vision.

This Ritual can be done in imagination or it can be done in actuality using the Ritual of the stones for the basis. It is a Ritual that can enter all aspects of your life on a daily basis.*

*This material is adapted from a lecture by Angeles Arrien.

I am circling around God, around the ancient tower, and I have been circling for a thousand years, and I still don't know if I am a falcon, or a storm, or a great song.
Rainer Maria Rilke

CHANTING & SINGING

In the dark time
Will there also
Be singing?
Yes, there will
Also be singing
About the dark times.
Berthold Brecht

Many cultures around the world use singing and chanting to help them with their grieving. Gregorian chants and gospel songs are Christian forms familiar to many of us. The bhajans and chants of Buddhists and Hindus, and the calls of the Moslem muezzins are related to forms familiar to many others. When we are grieving, it is often helpful to us in our grief to chant or sing. Find a chant, a song, or a hymn that speaks to your innermost place of feeling. Find a place where you will feel free to sing or chant, and do so. I know some people who sought out a gospel congregation, others who found a local ashram, and yet another person who sat at her piano and sang "Amazing Grace" over and over as a grieving Ritual. You may have a favorite tape that evokes the memories about the one you are grieving for. Yes, it may be painful, but the only way to heal the pain is to **feel** it. You may also be interested to know that the resonance created by music allows your body to come more fully into balance.

THE STONE CEREMONY

This is an ancient shamanic ritual that can be used for a number of purposes such as a commitment ceremony, a naming ceremony, and, in this instance, a grief work ceremony. You need to go either in actuality or in your mind's eye to a place where there are many stones and rocks. A river bank, a beach, or the edge of a mountain are good places to go. When you get there, walk around until you find the right place for your ceremony. Then begin by drawing a circle with a stick. The size of the circle is up to you, and a standard size is about as wide as you are tall. You need to be able to stand in the center of the circle. Now start by calling to the person or the event for whom you are grieving to come and be in the circle with you. Feel your feelings as you do this. Now go out of the circle and find four stones — one for each of the four directions in your circle. With the first stone, face the south from the center and tell the stone the feelings you have for the child-of-the-past in your lost friend. Tell the stone how you feel about that little child in them. When you have completed

Learn to look with an equal eye upon all beings, seeing the one Self in all.

Srimad Bhagavatam

this part, place the stone at the south end of the circle.
Now get another stone and face the west with the
stone. Talk to your stone about the friend you have
lost and about the warrior-like or valiant qualities
you saw in your friend. Tell the stone all of your feelings about this aspect of the person who was in your
life — feel all of your feelings. Do the same thing
with the third rock, facing the north and telling the
third rock how you appreciated the friend for his/her
mastery in life. Feel your feelings about this aspect
of your lost friend. Now with the fourth rock, face
the east and tell the rock about the vision your friend
had, and how your friend was a visionary in life. Feel
your feelings about this. Move now to the center of
the circle and sit there thanking your friend for
his/her contribution to your life. When you are done,
take each stone, thanking it for helping you in your
ritual and replace it where you found it. As much as
possible leave the area you used in the same state
you found it.

GOOD GRIEF TOTEM
COLLAGE OR
TREASURE MAP

Formation,
transformation,
Eternal Mind's
eternal re-creation.
Goethe, *Faust*

This Ritual will be fun and fulfilling, and if done appropriately it will be evocative and will help you in releasing some of the grief you have been carrying. Start by collecting a large stack of old magazines. I like the *National Geographic* and some of the travel magazines, and I know that almost any magazine will work. The other supplies you need are a pair of scissors, some glue stick, and a large piece of construction paper or a piece of cardboard. Start with going through the magazines as fast as you can. Do not use the thinking part or your brain, just the feeling part. Now start cutting out pictures, words, sayings, and captions that are evocative and remind you of the situation or the person for whom you are grieving. Continue this cutting-out process for about fifteen minutes. You can take longer if you wish, but the faster and more intuitively you do this, the more deeply it will speak to you later.

When you have your pile of pictures, captions, and words, then start to glue them to the large piece of paper. Put the person or item you have lost in the middle of the paper and then glue the other items around in whatever order seems to be satisfying to you. When you finish you will have a totem or treasure map for yourself that will symbolize all of the wonderful thoughts and feelings you have for the lost one. You will also have a decorative piece to hang on your refrigerator or your bathroom wall where you can look at it daily and continue your grief work by means of this creative and inspirational collage.

DREAM ANALYSIS

*Dreamer, it is I who am your dream —
Would you awake, I am your will.*
Rainer Maria Rilke

One of the ways to deal with grief is to analyze the dreams you are having during your grieving period. The following is a tried and true method for you to work with your own dreams and to find out what some of your deeper feelings are and what the message of the dream is for you. This works best as a writing exercise:

STEP ONE: Identify the two words that describe the dream: 1. *Feeling Word* (mad, sad, scared, glad, etc.) 2. *Action Word* (running, fighting, frozen, jumping etc.)

STEP TWO: Write the dream out in the first person present tense in two or three sentences; i.e., condense the dream. Now write out the long and detailed version of the dream.

STEP THREE: Be/speak from the other parts of the dream: e.g. I am the chair in my dream...; I am the man in my dream....

STEP FOUR: Enter the dream and find the place where you have the most energy — the person or object that is the most compelling to you right now.

STEP FIVE: Go into the dream and face the most compelling part/person/object, and say: 1. "What are you doing in my dream?" — get an answer! 2. "Who are you? — take off your mask!" Write out your feelings at this point and write out the answers to the questions.

STEP SIX: Face the unmasked one, and say: 1. "Will you be my friend or ally?" 2. "Give me something that will be symbolic of your willingness to be my friend." Write about this and **tell your feelings, feel your feelings**.

STEP SEVEN: Go over the dream and rewrite it to your satisfaction; i.e., change all the parts to your satisfaction, paint a different picture.

STEP EIGHT: In your life go on a quest to find that object given to you as a symbol of the ally in your dream so you can have a reminder of what your "scary part" gave you.

Memory is valuable for one thing, astonishing; it brings dreams back.
Antonio Machado

ANCHORING THE GOOD FEELINGS

Often when we are feeling sad it is hard to remember that we ever felt good. With a little effort we can re-call events in our lives when we were content, happy, had fun, or such. Find yourself in a quiet place where you will not be distracted, and let your mind wander to a time and a place when you felt good. Let it be a time not associated with the loss you're dealing with, but a time when you were genuinely in your own right pleased. In your mind's eye go to that event, see the colors and the objects, feel what it felt like to be there. Intensify that experience and the good feeling associated with it, and at the same time hold on to the small finger on your left hand, tight. Take a deep breath. Insert those good feelings into that little fin-ger. Anchor them there. Now release the finger and be with the good feelings for a moment. Go now to another event where you felt good and do the same thing as above, seeing, hearing, feeling, experiencing the event, and insert that feeling into the second fin-ger on your left hand.

Anchor It There. You can do this for all your fingers if you wish. So you have a good feeling anchored to your body, you can use your ear lobes, the end of your nose, any part of your body you can touch will work for this exercise. The next time you are feeling sad and do not have time to deal with it, reach for one of the fingers that is an anchor for you. You will surprise and delight yourself with what happens! A note of caution: this is not a substitute for doing the grief work. It is a helper, motivator, and useful for those who have to bracket their grieving and plan to get to it later.

TOTEM ANIMAL SPIRITS

The value of the personal relationship to all things is that it creates intimacy and intimacy creates understanding and understanding creates love.

Anais Nin

The animal spirit that offers itself to you as an ally is a helpful guardian and guide in times of grief. These are *power animals*, and they are pleased to be in a relationship with the human who calls to them for help. Animals, like rocks, have powerful spirits and very special talents that can be called upon in times of stress. To carry out this Ritual you will need to be in a quiet place where you will not be disturbed. If you have a drumming tape, use it to take you on your journey. The mental journey starts with finding your entry into the lower world. This is usually a crevice, a hole in the ground, a hollow tree, a cave, or other such place; allow yourself to go down into the Earth Mother; follow the path down until a landscape opens up before you. As you move through the landscape allow the image of animal, bird, or reptile to enter the landscape. You may not always see the exact animal. It may be a symbol of the animal like a statue or a belt buckle.

When the animal appears, ask it to tell you its special qualities. Listen: ask the animal to give you the particular assistance you are seeking in this grief period. Take its advice to heart. Thank it for its help and return to normal waking consciousness. Do not worry if it seems that you are making up the whole thing. You can continue to experiment with this process, meeting with your totem animal spirit as many times as you need to. If the animal that presents itself to you is hostile in any way, recognize this as an obstacle to be dealt with at another time. Power animal spirits are very helpful and useful sources of comfort and assistance, and it is important to honor them and to recognize them in various ways in order to keep them working for you.*

Be still, and let the dark come upon you Which shall be the darkness of God.

T.S. Eliot

---

* This Ritual, which is not so simple as others in this book, is what Shamans do as "Journeying," traveling in a trance state. If you wish to do this sort of work, you should begin with Sandra Ingerman's *Soul Retrieval* (Harper Collins: San Francisco, 1991) or Michael Harner's *The Way of the Shaman* (Harper & Row: San Francisco, 1990).

THE MAGIC SHOP

You are invited to find a quiet place somewhere where you will not be interrupted for fifteen to twenty minutes. Take a deep breath and let your mind wander to that city, town, or village that is your most favorite place in the whole world. See yourself walking down the main thoroughfare of this city, town, or village, and, as you walk, notice it is a fine day. It is spring, and the trees are budding and you are enjoying the good feeling of being in one of your favorite places. As you walk along, you will notice a small shop tucked way back between other buildings, its windows are dusty, and you do not remember seeing it before. You approach it and peer inside, there you see all kinds of things you have never imagined seeing in one place. It is the sort of wonderful junk shop, flea market, antique shop, and specialty shop all rolled into one. You open the door and notice way in the back a very **Wise Old Person** who feels quite familiar to you.

This Wise Old Person tells you that this is a place where you can realize your dreams if you wish. What you have to do is to select an item from the shop that is symbolic of some status or change you wish to accomplish in your life. In its place you may leave an old habit, feeling, job, person, or grief issue you no longer wish to have in your life.

Since this is a magic shop, anything can be taken in exchange for anything you wish to leave. You are told to take your time looking around for just the right symbol, and also to think carefully about what it is you wish to leave behind that is dysfunctional or painful to you. Take a few minutes now to wander around the shop looking at all of the wonderful items and mulling over what it is you wish to leave behind in exchange. When you are ready, put your unwanted item on the shelf, and take in its place the item you most want to symbolize this change you are about to make in your life. Take a few minutes to talk with the Wise Old Person and tell him/her what it is that you are leaving behind and what it is you are taking in its place. The Wise Old Person tells you that you have three weeks to change your mind, if you want the old habit, behavior, grief issue, etc. back, you can come back and return your new found item and retrieve the old. This is because it is sometimes scary for people to give up the old and familiar, and also they need more time to think about it before giving it up entirely. When you are done, thank the Wise Old Person and leave the shop finding yourself back in your favorite village, town, or city. Walking down the street, allow yourself slowly and easily to come back to present waking reality.

In the days and weeks ahead, allow yourself to find the item you took from the Magic Shop, perhaps at a flea market, in your grandmother's attic, or in an antique shop. Acquire the item as a concrete symbol that you are accomplishing your goals in your life.

*Not enjoyment, and
not sorrow,
Is our destined end or
way;
But to act, that each
tomrrow
Find us farther than
today.*

Longfellow

BLACK VELVET MEDITATION

Put yourself in a safe, quiet place where you will not
be interrupted or disturbed. Sit, or lie quietly for a
few moments following your breath. Notice how
your breath goes in and then out in a regular, predictable rhythm. After about ten breaths, begin to imagine yourself to be folded into layers and layers of soft
black velvet. Feel the softness and the comfort of the
black velvet and the quiet of the space you are occu-
pying. After about twenty breaths, allow yourself to
see a tiny little light in the black velvet that starts to
move towards you. Watch this little light become
larger as it approaches you, until you are totally surrounded with this light. You will begin to feel the
light as a source of all encompassing, deeply felt
unconditional love.

As you allow yourself to feel this love, allow yourself to remember that person whom you have lost, and feel their love for you surrounding you as the light now surrounds you. Feel your feelings about this person. Tell them anything you have not said and that still remains to be said. When you have felt the release from this experience, slowly allow yourself to come back into the black velvet, and finally back into the state of normal waking reality.

A WATERFALL

This is one of my favorite Rituals for self-cleansing and releasing the pain of loss. Find yourself in a quiet place and deepen your relaxation by following your breath, quietly and evenly. Imagine that you are walking through a deep forest on a mountain you have been climbing for some time. You notice the path has now turned into a gradual slope and you find yourself going down into a valley. As you climb down you become aware of your futility and pain. You feel deep sadness or anger at the loss you have suffered. You feel very burdened by your grief. It is a hot day and you are becoming very warm when you come upon a waterfall deep in the rocks, spilling into a wide pool. Listen to the sound of the splashing water. You remove your clothes and climb down into the water, feeling its cool, refreshing flow against your skin. Step under the waterfall and feel the water splashing down on your body and head.

As you stand there, allow the splashing water to pour down over your head and body, taking with it all of your pain, cares, and burdens. See and feel the pain washing out of your body, the water cleansing all of your sorrow. When you step out of the water, allow the sunshine to dry you and feel every cell and tissue in your body fill up with the sunlight until you feel full of light, refreshed and renewed. Reclothe yourself and retrace your steps bringing yourself back to the place in which you started your Ritual.

Move through transformation, out and in.
What is the deepest loss that you have suffered?
If drinking is bitter, change yourself to wine.
Rainer Maria Rilke

THE REFLECTIONS IN A POND

*Who comes to a spring
thirsty
and sees the moon
reflected in it?*

Rumi

Find yourself in a safe place and relax. Deepen your relaxation by breathing steadily and following your breath. Go now to a pond you know on a warm summer day. Enjoy the soft air, the breath of a small breeze, and the warmth of the sun as you walk towards your pond. Feel the grasses against your bare legs, listen to the birds, and smell the soft scent of the damp ground and grasses you have stepped on. Now bend over and look into the water of the pond and see there the reflection of your own face mirrored in the still water. Begin to notice the changes in your reflection as you gaze into the water, notice the memories, thoughts, feelings that are stimulated by this process. Think about the attitudes or behaviors or conditions in your life you would like to change.

Speak to that part of you that is holding on to the pain of your grief—speak gently, and feel the feelings that arise. Every now and then splash the water with your hand and sprinkle the water over you as you say: "I release myself from this pain." Do this several times. When you are complete with this process, return yourself to a state of awakeness and awareness, taking with you the cleansing and releasing that this Ritual offers you.

ACKNOWLEDGING OUR OWN MORTALITY

The end is where we start from.

T.S. Eliot

Many of us spend most of our lives denying that we are going to die some day. The energy we put into this denial prevents us from really fully enjoying our lives. Here is a Ritual you can set up so that you can explore the day of your dying. It is believed in many cultures that we decide how we are going to die and we can be in charge of the manner of our dying. In this exercise, allow yourself to Imagine the following:

It is the day of your dying some time in the future. You may imagine the setting: where is it you plan to die, will it be in your own bed, sitting in the rocker on the front porch, under your favorite tree, doing your favorite thing? You decide this in your fantasy. Then go to the setting in your mind's eye and allow yourself to see the place, the objects, the colors, and who is there to witness your dying. See yourself in the situation, sitting, lying, surrounded by these people, in

When we realize we are already dead, our priorities change, our hearts open, our mind begins to clear of the fog of old holdings and pretendings.

Stephen Levine

spirit or in the flesh, hear the sounds, and feel the feelings as your spirit leaves your body. Let yourself review the scene and ask yourself if that is how you really want it to be. Feel the feelings, and make any changes you wish to make. This is your death scene and you can have it anyway you wish. When you are finished, bring yourself back to normal waking Reality. You may want to write this experience — be sure to note the exact feelings.

NEAR DEATH EXPERIENCES

Birth and death are not two different states, but are different aspects of the same state.

Mahatma Gandhi

Many people have had these experiences, and their lives have profoundly changed afterwards. If you are one of these people, and because a number of years ago people did not talk about such things for fear of being considered "weird," you may not have fully acknowledged for yourself the importance of your experience. Allow yourself to recall this experience and to write about it and to fully experience the feelings associated with it. You may also wish to connect with a support group of people who have had similar experiences. There is an organization — International Association of Near Death Experiences — located in Stanford, Connecticut. They can put you in touch with a support group in your own city. If you have never had such an experience and have lost a loved one, you will find that the IANDS meetings are very comforting and can be a source of great support for you also.

THE CAPE OF GRIEF

I participated in this Ritual at a workshop many years ago. I find myself returning to it from time to time because of the light and joyful feeling I feel when I come out of the Ritual. I have seen it written up in a number of places and will give credit to being introduced to it in the early '70s by Will Schutz.

Start by relaxing yourself, and, when you are ready, imagine the garment you are wearing, a gown or a cape, as being very heavy, black, and uncomfortable. This is the garment of your grief. Pay attention to this heavy garment resting on your shoulders and pressing against your body. Feel how hot and oppressive the garment is to you. Feel the texture and coarseness of the cloth against your skin. Notice how deep your despair is. Stay with that deep discomfort for as long as you can stand it. Feel your feelings of *mad, sad, scared* until you believe that you are ready to be relieved of your grief, call on your higher self or your guides, or ask your God/Goddess to take this burden from you.

As it begins to lift from your shoulders and disappears over your head, you notice that your higher reality has provided you with a light delicate garment, which feels like a shower of stars pouring down over your body. Feel the many tiny points of light penetrating your body and note that you feel protected and filled with love and joy and a wonderful lightness. Enjoy the feeling and the wonderful lightness and make it fully yours so you can return to your garment of light anytime you wish. Now return to your usual waking reality.

For self is a sea boundless and measureless.

Kahlil Gibran

BETRAYAL

Love has earth to
which she clings.
Robert Frost

Often we find that *betrayal* is a big theme of the
major losses that we have encountered in our lives.
There are large betrayals and lesser betrayals. You
may want to have a tape recorder or a friend who will
bear witness to this Ritual. If you do not have a friend
readily available, you can use the tape recorder to
talk into as you do the Ritual. Now try going for a
walk into your past. You can actually take a walk, or
do it in your imagination. Allow yourself to go back
slowly in your life to recover the betrayals you have
felt. Let your remembrance, as you walk back through
your life, supply you with the list, sorting as you go,
put the larger betrayals on the left, and the lesser ones
on the right as you walk back through life. You will
recognize the larger ones as being those for which
you have a stronger gut response than the others.
Save the larger betrayals for later.

When you have recorded your responses to each of the lesser betrayals that have come to mind on your walk backwards in your life, then you may address the major betrayals. Tell the tape or your witness about these. When you have done this, tell the witness or the tape what the consequences were from these betrayals. After dealing with your feelings about these incidents, see if you can forgive those who betrayed you. If you cannot do this, make the gesture of forgiveness "as if" it were possible. This is a practice session for the future when you will be able to fully forgive. Now start to walk forward in your life, confronting each of the lesser betrayals and forgiving the transgression against you. After you have done this, spend some time reflecting on the experience of this Ritual.*

*This Ritual is adapted from Jean Houston, *Search for the Beloved* pp. 119-121.

MIND MAPPING

Take a piece of paper, and, in the middle of the paper, put the name of the person, object, or event representing the cause of your grief. Then draw a circle around the name and draw a line in any direction from the circle; then draw another circle in which you will write the first word that comes to mind in association with the previous word. Do three or four of these and go back to the main circle in the middle and draw another line with another circle and any association that comes to mind. An example below shows how I gained release from the death of my husband, Dick.

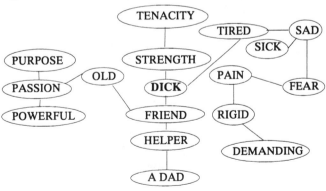

EVERY ENDING
IS A BEGINNING

The tomb looks just like a prison, but it's really a release into Union.

Rumi

Grief work is very detailed and meticulous work. It is not for the faint of heart, the deniers, or those who are not **one hundred percent** committed to their own growth process and to becoming clear of their past. It is a pathway to health and serenity. Grief work is the work of the soul or spirit. Those of us who aspire to "cleaning up" our past — our karma — and to becoming really clean and clear in our lives and in our dealings with all of the magnificent human beings it is our privilege to encounter in this brief lifetime **must do this work**. We must say what was left unsaid, and we must let ourselves hear what was not heard by those involved the first time. They do not have to be present to become clear within our own inner selves.

Do you remember the *stage* earlier in this book? Now I want you to return to it. Go up to each person who is now on the right side of the stage, and say **"I Love You,"** and **"I Am Grateful To You"** to each person.

GOODBYE, I AM GRATEFUL

The most minute transformation is like a pebble dropped into a still lake. The ripples spread out endlessly.

Emmanuel

As you embark on this journey of acknowledging your own magnificence and the Good Within and clearly come into your own, you will experience transformation in your life. You will find yourself increasingly grateful to those who have given you these lessons. Your life will fill with gratitude and light. You can take your time — take as long as you need to do this. I suggest that you set arbitrary time limits on each contract that you take out on those you are in the process of forgiving. The work will proceed in your subconscious when you are sleeping and when you are awake, and you will surprise and delight yourself with actually accomplishing the goals you have set, often meeting the deadlines you have agreed upon. Remember always that this is a meticulous and demanding process. It is often very hard work.

You are worth it.

You are a Child of the Universe,
a magnificent creature.
You are wanted and loveable.
You are now inviting into
your life the people,
events and situations
which are important to your destiny.
You deserve to be free of old pain.
You deserve to claim your birthright.
You are Good.

RELATED READINGS

Bishop, Jacqui and Grunte, Mary: *How to Love Yourself When You Don't Know How: Healing All Your Inner Children*. P.U.L.S.E/Station Hill. Barrytown, N.Y. 1992.

Bowlby, John: *Attachment and Loss,* Vols. I, II, III. Basic Books. New York. 1969.

Bozarth-Campbell, Alla: *Life is Goodbye: Life is Hello.* Camp Care Publications. Minnesota. 1982.

Childs-Gowell, Elaine: *Bodyscript Blockbusting*. Murray Publishing Company. Seattle. 1976.

Erskine, Richard and Zalcam, Marilyn: "The Racket System." *T.A. Journal,* Vol. 9, No. 1. 1979.

Haldane, Sean: *Emotional First Aid: A Crisis Handbook.* Station Hill. Barrytown, N.Y. 1988.

Ingerman, Sandra: *Soul Retrieval: Mending the Fragmented Self.* Harper Collins. San Francisco. 1991.

Justice, Blair: *Who Gets Sick?* Peak Press. Houston. 1987.

Kübler-Ross, Elizabeth: *Death, The Final Stage of Growth*. Prentice Hall. New Jersey. 1975.

Ray, Sondra: *I Deserve Love.* Les Femmes Publishing Company. San Francisco. 1976.

Rodegast, Pat and Stanton, Judith: *Emmanuel's Book.* Bantam Books. New York. 1985.

ABOUT THE AUTHOR

Elaine Childs-Gowell, RN, MN, MPH, Ph.D., completed her nursing degree at Yale University, her Public Health degree at Tulane University, and her Ph.D. in Anthropology at the University of Washington. She has been teaching, healing, counseling, and doing psychotherapy for more than 20 years. She is currently in private practice as a Shaman, healer, and Clinical Transactional Analyst in Seattle, working with individuals, couples, families, and groups. Elaine is well known in the Northwest, Canada, and Europe and in TA circles as a therapist and workshop leader, particularly through her work relating Transactional Analysis with the body, and in Corrective Parenting. She has created many workshops for healing grief and considers herself a "spiritual midwife."

How to Break the Vicious Circles in Your Relationships
A Guide for Couples

DEE ANNA PARRISH

The message of this clear and sympathetic book is that dysfunctional relationships characterized by a predictable pattern of vicious circles—can be healed. Reassuring case histories, drawn from the author's own therapeutic practice, demonstrate why relationships disintegrate, and show how they can be made whole again. Here are proven techniques designed to short-circuit destructive habits. Readers will learn to use "defusers" to keep conflicts from escalating, gauge levels of emotional intimacy and identify barriers to closeness, examine their own levels of communication and quality of listening, use "I" statements to identify problematic issues, and uncover inter-generational patterns of dysfunction. For anyone seeking to improve a relationship or reconnect with a partner—with or without the aid of a therapist—this is essential reading.

DEE ANNA PARRISH, a psychotherapist specializing in family and couple therapy, is the author of *ABUSED: A Recovery Guide for Adult Survivors of Physical/Emotional Abuse*. She lives in Dallas, Texas.

$8.95p, ISBN 0-88268-144-3

How to Forgive When You Don't Know How

Jacqui Bishop and Mary Grunte

In this groundbreaking look at the psychology of forgiveness, the authors show how resentment—toward other people, toward one's self, even toward God—can consume precious emotional energy and seriously impair both self-esteem and the ability to experience joy. Drawing on the healing techniques used so successfully in *HOW TO LOVE YOURSELF WHEN YOU DON'T KNOW HOW*, they offer a short program for accelerating the process of forgiveness, including visualization, emotional discharge, searching back, and prayer. Enlivened with classic quotations on the nature of forgiveness, this revolutionary book explodes long-standing myths—including the notion that forgiveness involves self-denial, making up, confessing, or turning the other cheek.

JACQUI BISHOP and MARY GRUNTE are the authors of *HOW TO LOVE YOURSELF WITH YOU DON'T KNOW HOW: Healing All Your Inner Children*. A psychologist and psychiatric nurse respectively, they both live in White Plains, New York.

$7.95p, ISBN 0-88268-142-7

How to Love Yourself When You Don't Know How

Healing All Your Inner Children

JACQUI BISHOP & MARY GRUNTE

The notion that each of us carries around an inner child has been widely explored in popular psychology; this groundbreaking book takes the premise one step further, describing an interior model for the individual based on the metaphor of the family. Everyone, say the authors, is really made up of an inner family—several children of various ages and characters, each of who vies for control in one's life, as well as an inner grown-up capable of learning to care for them. The book's aim is to help the reader re-educate the inner grownup to love unconditionally, opening the way for profound healing of psychic wounds.

$10.95 paper, ISBN 0-88268-131-1, 6 x 9, bibliography, index.

Abused

A Guide to Recovery for Adult Survivors of Emotional/Physical Child Abuse

DEE ANNA PARRISH, MSSW

This clear and sensitively written book covers child abuse in all its forms, including types of abuse overlooked by the victims themselves: neglect, deprivation, ridicule, and inappropriate sexual gestures. *Abused* includes a wealth of revealing and highly moving first-person accounts, a program for recovery, a resource directory, and various self-tests to help readers determine if they once were abused and today need counselling or therapy. It includes a parents' guide to behavioral signs of sexual abuse plus the first guide to describe techniques used by therapists to uncover repressed memories. Illustrated with case histories, *Abused* is written for adults who suspect the treatment they received as children still impairs their sense of judgment and well-being today.

$8.95 paper, ISBN 0-88268-089-7, 6 x 9, 150 pages, bibliography, resource guide, index.

Emotional First Aid
A Crisis Handbook
SEAN HALDANE, M.D.

Emotional First Aid is the first book to address immediate emotional crisis as distinct from a person's general state of mental health. It deals with grief, anger, fear, joy, and also the complex feelings of parent/child conflicts—emotions that can lead to further withdrawal, illness, or even violence. Clear and extraordinarily well written, this is the frist book to draw on Reichian character analysis to explain how differences in individuals and in specific emotions call for different responses, if one is to be supportive and not invasive. Emotional first aid may precede or prevent therapy in the same way that physical first aid can precede or prevent extended medical treatment.

$9.95 paper, ISBN 0-88268-071-4, 6 x 9, 160 pages, bibliography, index.

Sam Woods
American Healing
STAN RUSHWORTH

This unusual and eloquent book is not about healing technique, but is an extraordinary exploration into the healing spirit. Weaving together prayers and stories, Sam Woods reveals a fascinating world of healings, revelation and discovery through healing, and attitudes toward healing; the book becomes a healing unto itself as we begin to feel and see the way Sam Woods moves through his life. With prayer and praise, illumination and judgment, a healer's view of living today is opened to us, and we see how we are drawn to fall away from the Earth, and how we come back.

Sam Woods says, "This book is a joining, a listening to the voices of the earth, of the hawk and frog, of the children, of the people. It is a long prayer, a gathering together, a quiet walk into seeing, carrying everything with us as we go, our history, our ancestors, our sorrow, and our promise."

$11.95 paper, ISBN 0-88268-122-2, 5½ x 8½, 292 pages.